THE HISTORY OF IRELAND

Written by
Richard Tames

Designed by
Maureen and Gordon Gray

Illustrated by
Robin Lawrie

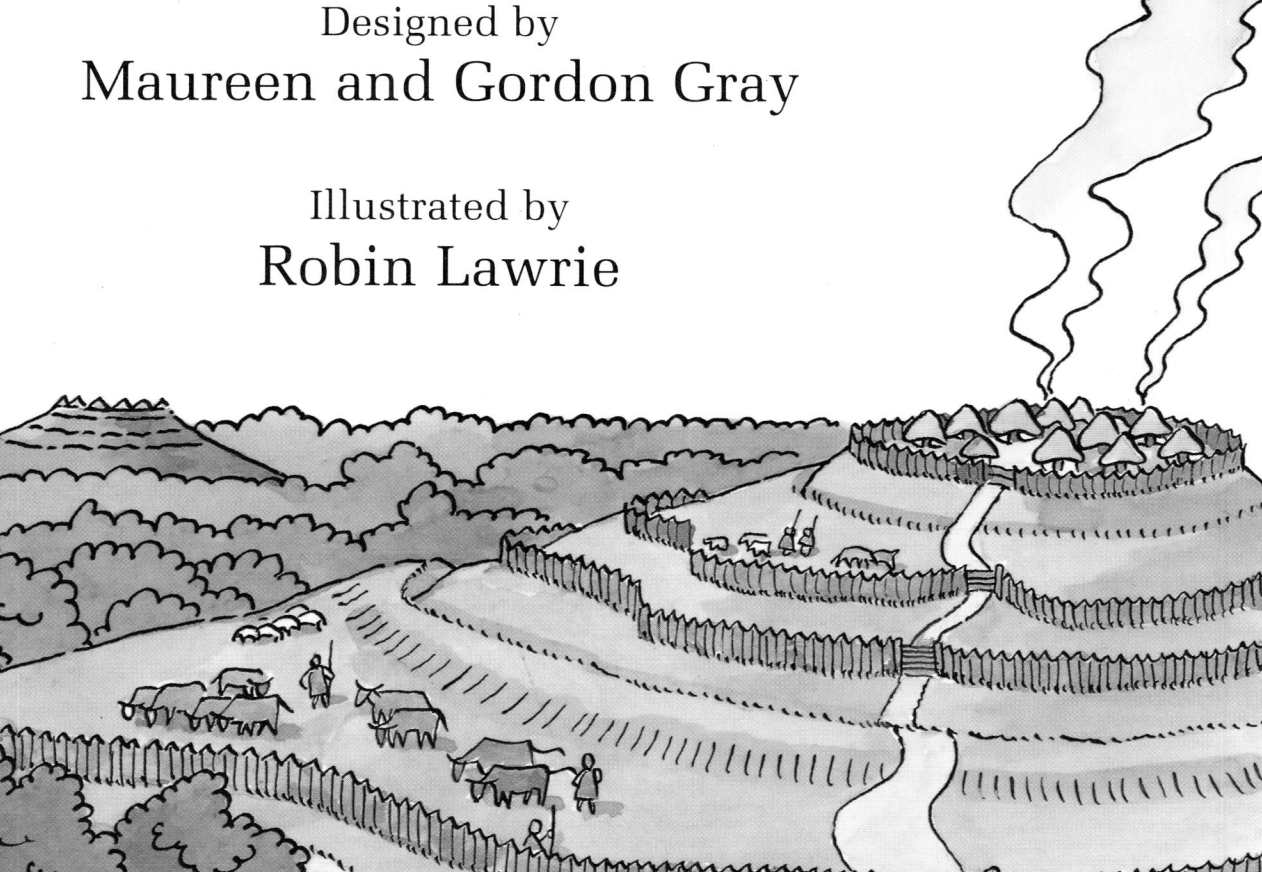

Gill & Macmillan

About this book

This edition published
in Ireland by
Gill & Macmillan Ltd
Goldenbridge
Dublin 8
with associated
companies throughout
the world.

Edited by: Paul Harrison
and Eveleen Coyle
Consultant:
Yvonne Carroll
Director of Editorial:
Jen Green
Editorial Manager:
Hazel Songhurst
Senior Editor:
Philippa Moyle
Production: Zoë Fawcett &
Simon Eaton
Series Concept:
Tony Potter
Cover Illustrator:
Robin Lawrie
Timeline design by
Chrissie Sloan
Timeline illustration by:
Kim Woolley

This book was created
and produced by
Zigzag Publishing Ltd,
The Barn, Randolph's Farm,
Hurstpierpoint,
West Sussex BN6 9EL,
Great Britain

Colour separations by Master
Image, Hong Kong
Printed by New Interlitho, Italy

Copyright © 1995
Zigzag Publishing Ltd

ISBN 0 7171 2325 1

10 9 8 7 6 5 4 3 2 1

The history of Ireland is a fascinating story of struggles and heroism. This book tells you all about the people who have made Ireland the country that it is today.

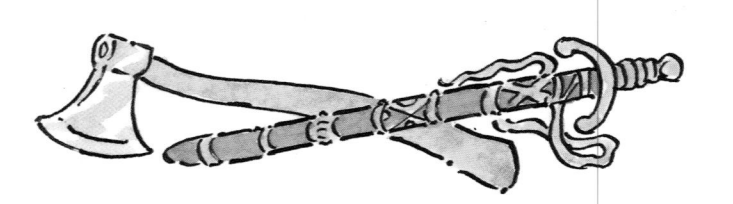

Discover the events that have changed the course of Irish history. Find out about Ireland's first settlers, what happened to the people who emigrated to America, and why Ireland was divided.

The illustrated Timeline that runs through the book shows you the developments and inventions that have changed the world from earliest times to the present day.

AD 1050 Sailors in Europe find their way using astrolabes.

AD 1065 Stained glass is fitted in the windows of Augsburg Cathedral in Germany.

AD 1066 A huge comet appears. It is later called Halley's Comet.

AD 1066 William the Conqueror becomes King of England.

AD 1086 The Domesday Book is completed.

Contents

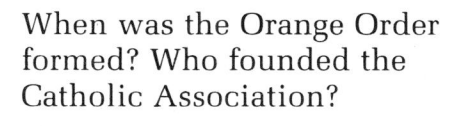
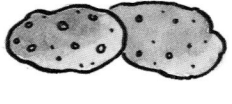

Celts

Ireland's first settlers probably came from Scotland around 8000 BC. They were hunters and fishermen who lived near the sea and rivers. Later, settlers moved further inland and began to farm the land. They learned how to make metal weapons, tools and jewellery.

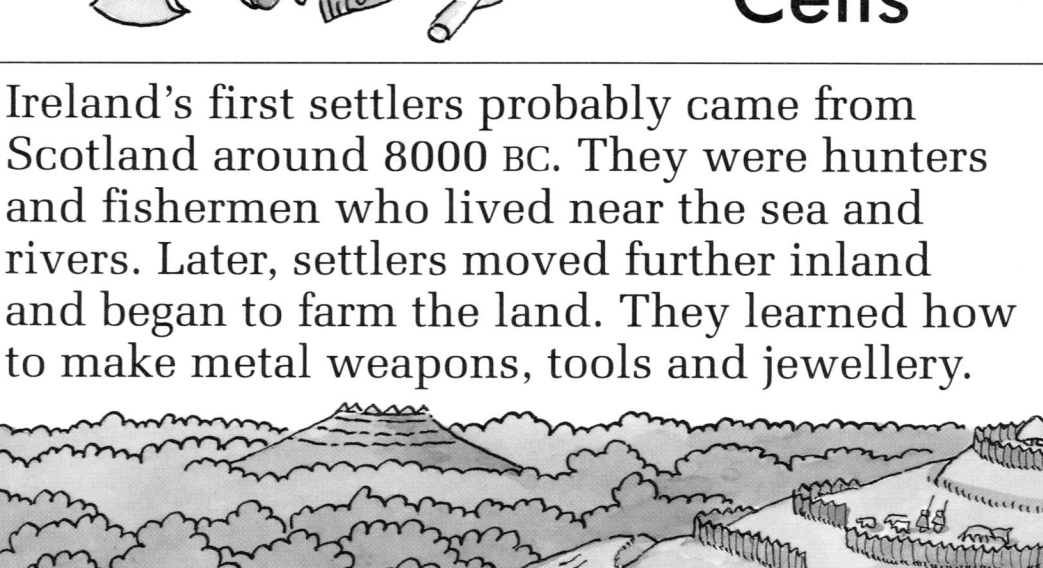

Safety first!

The early settlers lived in small groups of families and tribes. As they often fought each other and stole each other's cattle and slaves, the need for protection was great. Some people protected themselves by building forts on high ground. Others lived on islands in rivers or lakes, and were defended by water. Sometimes people even built artificial islands, called crannógs.

Invaders!

Around 250 BC, Ireland began to be invaded by Celts from mainland Europe. The most powerful group of Celts was called the Gaeil. By AD 400 they had conquered all of the other tribes. Everyone began to speak their language – Gaelic.

8000 BC People start to grow crops. The first known farming town is Jericho, in Israel.

7000 BC Clay pots are used for storing food and drink.

6000 BC The fibres of plants and the fleece of sheep and goats are used to make clothing.

6000 BC Bricks are used for building.

5000 BC People dig irrigation ditches from rivers to water their crops.

4500 BC People fish with hooks in the Black Sea.

Travel and trade

There were no roads and few wheeled vehicles. Some goods were carried by packhorse but it was usually easier to use dugout canoes on rivers and lakes. For sea travel people used boats made from wicker frames and hides, called curraghs. Traders would travel to Britain to exchange Irish copper for Cornish tin. When these two metals are mixed together they make bronze.

Who's who

Apart from the tribal kings, the most important people were priests (druids), poets (filí), musicians (bards), lawyers (brehons) and smiths. There was no money and the richest people were the ones with the most cattle.

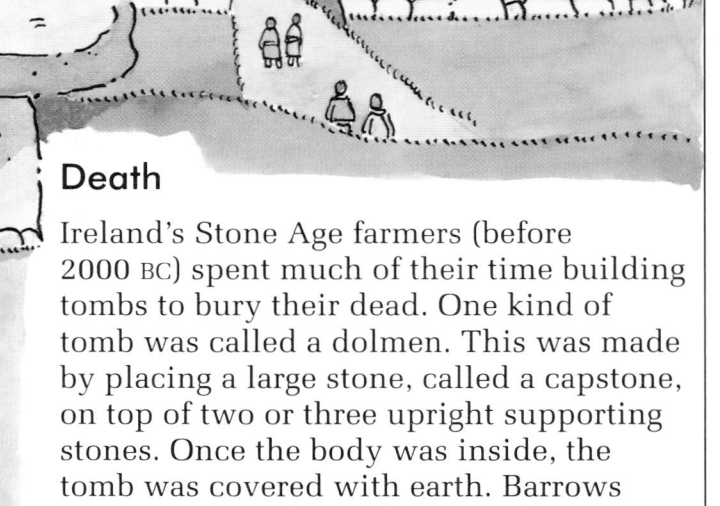

Death

Ireland's Stone Age farmers (before 2000 BC) spent much of their time building tombs to bury their dead. One kind of tomb was called a dolmen. This was made by placing a large stone, called a capstone, on top of two or three upright supporting stones. Once the body was inside, the tomb was covered with earth. Barrows were larger tombs, and were either long, round or wedge-shaped. They often had passages leading to a burial chamber in the middle. It would take a hundred men a month to build a barrow.

The Five Fifths

Ireland was divided into about 150 little kingdoms, called tuatha. These slowly combined into five groups called the Five Fifths. They were Ulaid (Ulster), Midhe (Meath), Laigin (Leinster), Muma (Munster) and Connacht (Connaught).

ULAID
MIDHE
CONNACHT
LAIGIN
MUMA

3600 BC Tin is mixed with copper to make bronze. It makes better tools and weapons.

3200 BC Picture writing appears in Mesopotamia.

3200 BC Carts are fitted with solid wooden wheels in Mesopotamia.

3000 BC The Egyptians use cloth to make clothes.

3000 BC A board game is played in Mesopotamia.

2000 BC People in Egypt use shadow clocks to tell the time.

Christianity

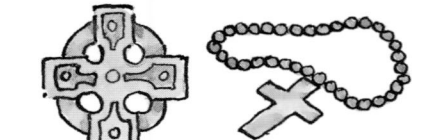

The coming of Christianity to Ireland, around AD 431, put people closer in touch with the rest of Europe. Ireland became a land of respected saints and scholars. These scholars were the first people to write down Irish legends, laws and history.

St Patrick

Patrick was probably born in Wales around AD 385, the son of a Roman official. As a boy, he was carried off to Ireland by pirates and became a slave. After six years, he escaped from Ireland and became a monk. He returned to Ireland to teach people about the Christian religion. After he died, he became the patron saint of Ireland.

Holy book

The Book of Kells is one of Europe's greatest treasures. It is a beautiful copy of the Four Gospels, illustrated with wonderfully detailed pictures. It was probably written around AD 800 at the monastery at Kells, County Meath.

Monasteries

As there were no towns, monasteries became major centres of learning. There were over 800 monasteries, the most important of which was at Clonmacnoise, County Offaly. Missionaries went out from these monasteries to preach and teach all over Europe. Monasteries also had to be made safe from Viking raids. Monks did this by building tall stone towers which could only be entered by climbing up a ladder. This could be pulled up if raiders attacked.

1500 BC The Hittites of Turkey heat ore with wood to make iron.

1300 BC The first alphabet, with each letter as a single sound, appears in Syria.

eee!

1000 BC Scissors made of bronze are used in Asia.

700 BC In Mesopotamia, concrete is made to build a canal.

700 BC The King of Lydia, in Ancient Greece, makes the first coins.

510 BC The first known map of the world is drawn by a Greek mapmaker.

St Columba

Columba was born in Ireland in AD 521. After he had founded monasteries at Derry and Durrow, he founded one on the island of Iona in the Inner Hebrides, a group of islands off the coast of Scotland. Irish monks from Iona took Christianity to Scotland. Columba is said to have written out 300 books by hand!

Brian Boru

Brian Boru was a powerful warlord who defeated his rivals to become the first king of all Ireland. In 1014, the men of Leinster joined the Vikings and rose up against Brian, but were defeated at the Battle of Clontarf. Brian was killed during the battle and Ireland became divided again.

Vikings

Vikings came from Scandinavia in longships to attack Irish monasteries, and steal treasure, such as gold crosses and church decorations. They also built bases along the coast which were used as trade centres. These bases became the first Irish towns. The most important were Dublin, Wexford, Waterford, Wicklow, Cork and Limerick.

500 BC
The quill pen is made from a sharpened feather.

350 BC
The Romans begin to build roads from one end of their empire to the other.

300 BC Pulleys are used for lifting heavy objects.

285 BC The first lighthouse is built off the coast of Egypt.

100 BC The Romans invent central heating for houses.

70 BC The Romans use water-wheels to grind grain and crush olives to make oil.

Normans

For over 150 years after the death of Brian Boru, rival warlords fought each other to become king of all Ireland. After Dermot MacMurrough lost the throne of Leinster, he invited Norman warriors from England to help him to get it back. These allies soon took most of Ireland for themselves.

Strongbow

From 1169 onwards, Norman armies landed in Ireland. Richard de Clare, the Earl of Pembroke, or Strongbow as he was known, was their most important leader. He formed an alliance with Dermot MacMurrough and married his daughter, Aoife. The Normans soon conquered Dublin and all the east coast towns. Strongbow even became king of Leinster after Dermot's death.

Henry II

King Henry II of England was worried about his Norman nobles setting up their own kingdoms in Ireland. In 1171, he visited Ireland with a large army. The Norman nobles and the Irish kings swore allegiance to Henry and agreed that he should be their overlord.

The Pale

By 1250, the Normans had conquered three-quarters of Ireland, including most of the best land. The area around Dublin became the heart of English royal power and was known as the Pale. The Normans protected their conquests by building castles, such as Carrickfergus in County Antrim, and walled towns, such as Carlow. Irish people were not supposed to live in the new towns.

NEW TOWN
Keep out

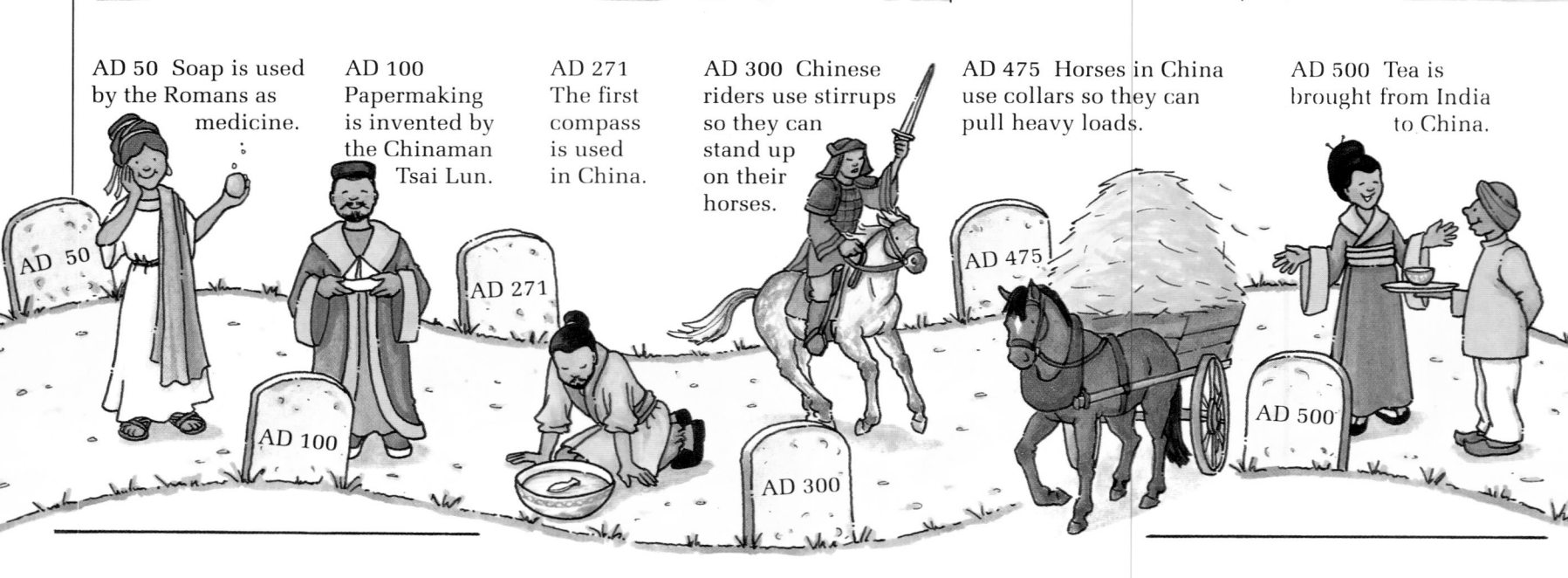

AD 50 Soap is used by the Romans as medicine.

AD 100 Papermaking is invented by the Chinaman Tsai Lun.

AD 271 The first compass is used in China.

AD 300 Chinese riders use stirrups so they can stand up on their horses.

AD 475 Horses in China use collars so they can pull heavy loads.

AD 500 Tea is brought from India to China.

AD 50

AD 100

AD 271

AD 300

AD 475

AD 500

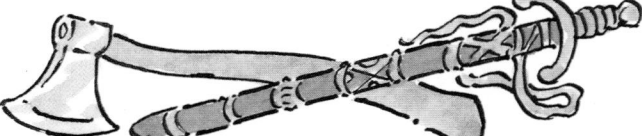

Richard II

King Richard II of England came to Ireland in 1394-5 and in 1399. He wanted to defeat Art MacMurrough Kavanagh, a troublesome Gaelic lord, who raided the southern borders of the Pale. Richard failed completely. English power was becoming very weak in Ireland. Even the Pale had shrunk to only a few miles around Dublin.

Revival

The Irish soon learned Norman methods of warfare, and hired soldiers from Scotland to fight on their side against the Norman nobles. As the English were busy fighting the French in the Hundred Years War, they could not send soldiers to help the Norman nobles. By the 1300s, large areas in the north and west of Ireland had returned to Irish rule. Even in the south and east where the Normans still ruled, the links with England were being broken as the nobles were marrying Irish people and speaking Gaelic. In 1366, laws were passed to stop Normans from marrying Irish people, wearing Irish clothes or speaking Gaelic. Most people ignored these laws.

AD 550 Early forms of chess are played in India.

AD 600 The Slavs of Eastern Europe invent a plough which can cut heavy soil.

AD 700 The first windmill appears in Persia.

AD 700 Mills driven by water-wheels are used in Europe.

AD 748 Printed newspapers appear in China.

AD 750 Beds become common in France and Germany.

Tudor times

During the 1400s, Ireland was controlled by three great Irish noble families. The Earl of Desmond ruled the far south-west, the Earl of Ormonde the centre, and the Earl of Kildare the east. By the late 1500s, the English were sending armies and settlers to Ireland to try to strengthen their position.

Earl of Ormonde

Earl of Kildare

Earl of Desmond

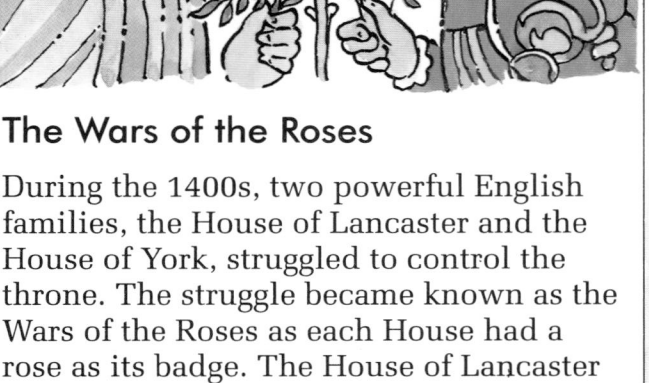

The Wars of the Roses

During the 1400s, two powerful English families, the House of Lancaster and the House of York, struggled to control the throne. The struggle became known as the Wars of the Roses as each House had a rose as its badge. The House of Lancaster had a red rose and the House of York a white rose. The wars lasted for over 60 years, and, as a result, English attention was diverted away from Ireland.

The Kildares

The Fitzgerald family owned huge estates and were intermarried to all the important Irish families. In 1470, Thomas Fitzgerald, 7th Earl of Kildare, was made chief governor of Ireland. As chief governor, Fitzgerald was expected to use his army to maintain order for the English. However, the Kildares became very powerful and ruled Ireland like kings for over half a century. English kings tried twice, unsuccessfully, to make someone else chief governor, until Henry VIII came to the throne. Henry imprisoned the Earl of Kildare in the Tower of London, where he died in 1536.

AD 760 Arabic numbers, the ones we use today, appear in Baghdad.

AD 765 Picture books are printed by hand in Japan.

AD 770 Horseshoes are used in Europe, allowing horses to travel further.

AD 802 The first rose trees are planted in Europe.

AD 850 An Ethiopian goatherd discovers coffee berries.

AD 868 The first printed book, *The Diamond Sutra*, is published in China.

AD 760

AD 765

AD 770

AD 802

AD 850

AD 868

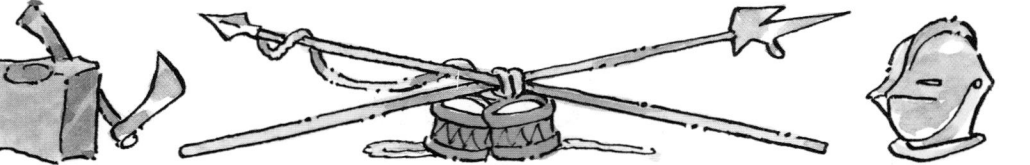

Henry VIII

In 1534, Henry decreed that all Irish land belonged to him and all Irish landowners were forced to surrender their lands to him. In return for the landowners' loyalty Henry regranted the land back. This was known as surrender and regrant.

In 1537, Henry broke the power of the Fitzgeralds for ever, when Silken Thomas, Fitzgerald's son, was executed in London after leading a failed rebellion. Henry later became the first English king to call himself King of Ireland, being the first to have complete control over the country.

English settlers

In 1557, the Irish parliament passed two laws allowing English settlers to take land in Ireland. The first English settlers arrived in the 1550s during the reign of Henry's daughter, Mary. More came later under her sister, Elizabeth I.

Religion and rebellion

As Queen Elizabeth I was a Protestant, and the Irish were mainly Catholic, it was unlikely that the Irish would remain loyal to a Protestant English ruler.

In the 1560s, there were rebellions in Munster, and Shane O'Neill led a rebellion in Ulster. All of these uprisings were defeated.

AD 900 Nobles begin to live in castles all over Europe.

AD 942 Good quality wool and linen cloths are made in Flanders.

AD 950 The Chinese use gunpowder for fireworks.

AD 963 A wooden bridge is built across the River Thames, the first London Bridge. Later ones, like this, were made of brick.

AD 969 Playing cards are used in China.

AD 996 Cane sugar arrives in Europe from Egypt.

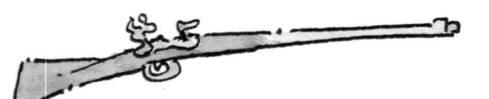
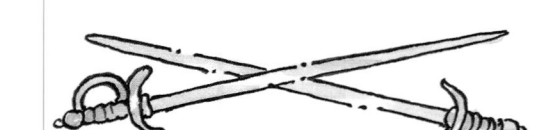

Irish dislike of the new settlers from England and Scotland led to all-out war in the 1590s. The Irish called on Spain, long-time enemy of England, for help, but were still defeated.

The struggle for Ulster

Hugh O'Neill, Lord of Tyrone, felt threatened by the settlers from England and Scotland. In 1594, English settlers took over Enniskillen Castle, an important stronghold from which they could take more of O'Neill's land.

Hugh O'Neill

Rebellion

In 1595, O'Neill led a rebellion to defend his estates against the settlers. As O'Neill and his army knew the area very well and the settlers did not, O'Neill was able to ambush them twice. However, O'Neill's men were unable to win an outright war with the English, so he sent a messenger to Spain asking for help.

King Philip III and Queen Margaret of Spain

Spain

Spain was the strongest Catholic country in Europe and the greatest enemy of Protestant England. As the English were helping Dutch rebels fight against Spanish rule in the Netherlands, King Philip III saw O'Neill's plea for help as a chance to get revenge. However, with the Spanish helping O'Neill, a war for land was also turned into a war of religion as well.

Catholic

Protesta

AD 1050 Sailors in Europe find their way using astrolabes.

AD 1065 Stained glass is fitted in the windows of Augsburg Cathedral in Germany.

AD 1066 A huge comet appears. It is later called Halley's Comet.

AD 1066 William the Conqueror becomes King of England.

AD 1086 The Domesday Book is completed.

AD 1090 A mechanical clock, driven by water, is built in Peking (now called Beijing).

Plantation

After the defeat of O'Neill's rebellion, the rebel's land was taken over by the English government. Ulster was then governed by English laws, not Gaelic ones. Over two million acres of the most fertile land in western Ulster were given to English and Scottish Protestants. This was known as the 'Plantation', as it was an attempt to plant, or settle, large numbers of people in Ulster.

Ulster

By 1618, there were 40,000 Scots in Ulster. They founded new towns and built proper roads. Many of the settlers grew very wealthy. If the Irish and the settlers had not been divided by religion they may have married one another and eventually become one people, but they remained separate. The Protestant settlers thought the Irish were backward and disloyal. The Catholic Irish thought that the settlers had given up the true religion and stolen their land.

Help and defeat

The Spanish army landed at Kinsale, in Munster, and were immediately trapped by the English. O'Neill marched south to free his allies and tried to make a surprise attack on the English on Christmas Eve 1601. O'Neill and the Spanish suffered a terrible defeat and the rebellion was a failure. Later, in 1607, O'Neill and other leading rebels fled to Europe. The last great Gaelic threat to England was gone.

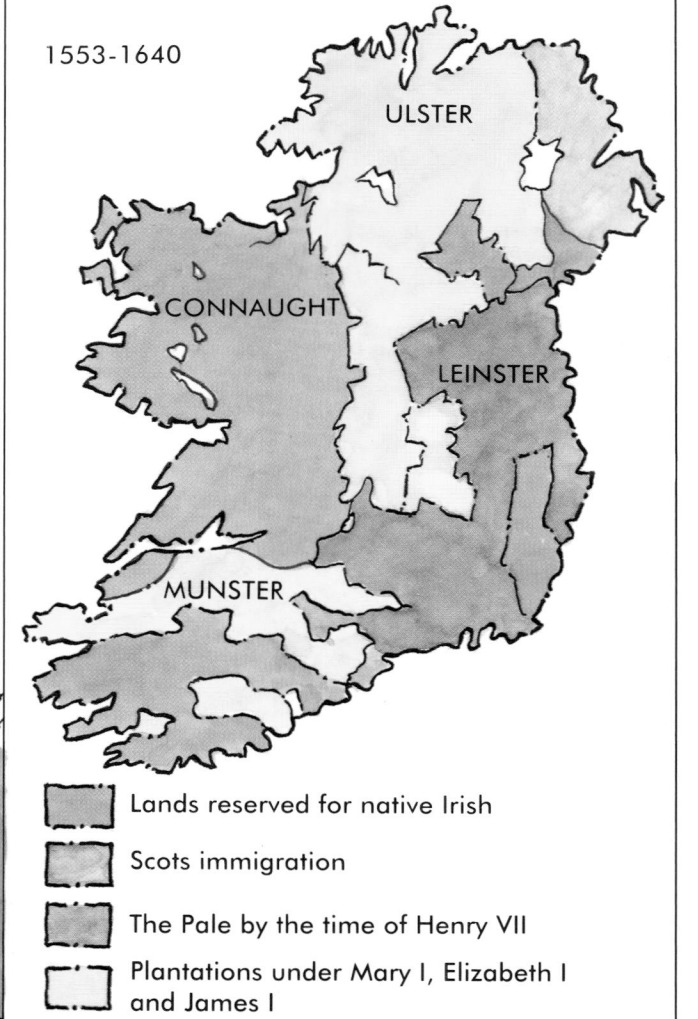

1553-1640

Lands reserved for native Irish

Scots immigration

The Pale by the time of Henry VII

Plantations under Mary I, Elizabeth I and James I

AD 1094 Gondolas are used as water taxis in Venice, Italy.

AD 1107 The Chinese print paper money using multicolour printing.

AD 1119 The University of Bologna is founded - the first university in Europe.

AD 1180 The first windmills with sails are built in Europe.

AD 1191 The Japanese learn to drink tea from the Chinese.

AD 1200 People begin to wear engagement rings.

The Protestant settlers were always afraid of an Irish uprising. Their fears were to be realised in 1641, when the English Civil War distracted English attention away from Ireland.

The Stuarts

Elizabeth I died in 1603, leaving no heir to the throne. James Stuart, already King James VI of Scotland, was Elizabeth's closest relative and became King James I of England. James oversaw the Plantation of Ulster and soon the Protestants controlled the Irish Parliament and Irish laws.

James I and his new coat of arms, which shows the Irish harp for the first time

Civil War

Charles I quarrelled with his Scottish subjects and asked Parliament for more money to raise an army against them.

Charles I

After James died in 1625, his son Charles became king. Charles, unable to raise taxes at home, sent the Earl of Strafford to Ireland to squeeze as much tax as possible out of both Protestant and Catholic Irish.

Instead of helping Charles, Parliament argued with him and this led to the English Civil War.

AD 1212 Work starts on Rheims Cathedral, in France.

AD 1215 King John signs the Magna Carta in England.

AD 1225 Cotton cloth is made in Spain.

AD 1232 The Chinese use kites to send messages during battles.

AD 1233 Coal is mined near Newcastle in England.

AD 1271 The explorer, Marco Polo, sets out on his overland journey to China.

Cromwell

Oliver Cromwell, leader of Parliament's forces, won the Civil War and had Charles executed in 1649. Cromwell then invaded Ireland and ruthlessly conquered it. At Drogheda and Wexford, thousands of Irish rebels were slaughtered. Many Catholics fled to Europe, or were sent to the West Indies to work on the plantations. Others were forced to move west of the River Shannon and live on poor land not wanted by the victorious Protestants – 'to Hell or to Connaught' as Cromwell stated. Around 11 million acres of land were taken from Catholic owners and given to Protestants.

Rebellion

The Catholic Irish landowners saw the Civil War as an excellent opportunity to regain their lost power. Protestant settlers were massacred and their churches destroyed. A Scottish army arrived to help the Ulster Protestants, but it was defeated by the Catholic rebels at Benburb in 1646. However, neither the Catholics nor the Protestants were strong enough to be completely victorious.

ULSTER

CONNAUGHT

LEINSTER

MUNSTER

1649-50

Lands reserved for native Irish

Lands reserved for Protestant settlement and veterans of Cromwell's army

Charles II and his mistress Nell Gwynne

Restoration

After Cromwell's death, England restored royal rule with Charles I's son, Charles II, as king. He was keen not to annoy Parliament and was content to leave Ireland alone.

AD 1278 Glass mirrors are invented.

AD 1285 Florence becomes the biggest business centre in Europe.

AD 1290 Spectacles are invented.

AD 1308 An indoor tennis court is built in Paris.

AD 1347 The Black Death kills a quarter of the people in Europe.

AD 1368 Rebuilding work begins on the Great Wall of China.

AD 1278

AD 1285

AD 1290

AD 1308

AD 1347

AD 1368

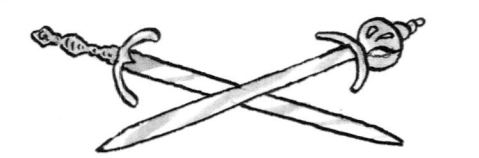

Protestant ascendancy

When James II came to the throne, it seemed that Catholic power might be revived, but the Williamite war ended this hope. Afterwards, Catholics faced many hardships under harsh Penal Laws.

A Catholic king

After Charles II died, his Catholic brother, James, became king. Irish and English Catholics welcomed the news of James II's coronation, but Protestants were suspicious of what he might try to do. The Protestants' fears were realised when James II gave Catholics important jobs in the government and the army, and when his wife produced a son to ensure the Roman Catholic succession.

Glorious Revolution

Leaders of Parliament who opposed James II invited the Dutch ruler, William of Orange, to land in England with an army, and rule with his wife, Mary. Mary was James' daughter, but unlike her father she was a Protestant. William and Mary landed in Britain and were crowned joint rulers. This event became known as the 'Glorious Revolution'. James II fled to Ireland to seek support.

The Williamite War

In Ireland, James II called a Parliament of Catholics which began to take power from the Protestant Church of Ireland and give land back to former Catholic landowners. He also led an army into Ulster, where the Protestants fled to the walled towns of Derry and Enniskillen. James II laid siege to Derry, a siege that lasted 105 days. The Protestants in Derry had so little to eat that they were forced to eat rats! The siege was finally broken when ships sent by William brought food to the starving city.

AD 1400 Blast furnaces are used to make cast iron.

AD 1405 Metal screws are invented.

AD 1415 Jan van Eyck discovers how to use oil paints.

AD 1455 Johann Gutenberg produces the first printed Bible.

AD 1464 A royal mail service is started in France by King Louis XI.

AD 1490 Leonardo da Vinci invents the parachute.

The Battle of the Boyne

On 1 July 1690, James II's and William's forces clashed at the Battle of the Boyne, the biggest battle fought in Ireland. William's army was victorious and James II fled to France. The fighting would continue for another year, but the Catholics were defeated. Many of their leaders and 10,000 soldiers fled to Europe – this was known as the 'Flight of the Wild Geese'. At the treaty of Limerick, which marked the end of the fighting, the Protestants promised to respect Catholic rights, but this was soon forgotten.

Prosperity and poverty

Ireland's Protestant rulers used their wealth to build fine country houses and made Dublin one of Europe's most attractive cities. However, this was in stark contrast to the lives of Ireland's rural Catholics, many of whom still spoke Gaelic and struggled to survive. In the 1740s, a famine led to the death of 300,000 from starvation and disease.

Penal Laws

For the next century, all power in Ireland was in the hands of the Protestants, who made up only one-tenth of the population. Under a system of strict laws, known as Penal Laws, Catholics were not allowed to vote, become lawyers or MPs, hold public office, go to university, join the navy or carry weapons. Many Catholics left Ireland to become successful soldiers or priests in Europe.

Dissenters

The Penal Laws also affected Protestants, for example Calvinists and Presbyterians, who were not members of the Church of Ireland. These people were known as Dissenters and many left Ireland to go to America rather than face prejudice.

AD 1490 Orphanages for children whose parents have died are opened in Italy.

AD 1490 The first ballets are performed for noblemen in Italy.

AD 1492 Christopher Columbus lands in the Bahamas, America, thinking he is in China.

AD 1492 Leonardo da Vinci draws plans for a flying machine.

AD 1497 Vasco da Gama sails around the southern tip of Africa on his way to India.

AD 1504 The first pocket watch is made in Germany.

Revolution

Unrest in the countryside and revolutionary ideas from abroad led to a number of failed uprisings. It was not until Daniel O'Connell united Irish Catholics in a peaceful struggle for their rights that they had any success.

Steps to reform

The British government wanted Irish Catholics to join its army in the fight against American independence and in other overseas campaigns. Britain hoped that reforms in favour of Catholics might end trouble in the countryside and help recruit loyal soldiers.

Last Will and Testament

I Seamus Doyle leave all my land and property to my eldest son Dominic Patrick Doyle. The cash in the storybox to be divided between my children.

Seamus Doyle

1779

Catholic Relief Act

In 1778, the Catholic Relief Act was passed to make it easier for Catholics to own land. After the French Revolution, fear of a similar event happening in Ireland led to other reforms to keep Catholics loyal to Britain.

Revolution!

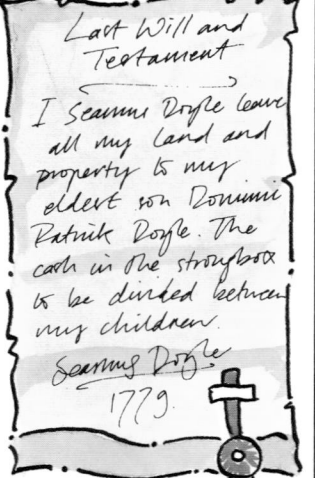

In 1791, a group of Ulster Dissenters formed the Society of United Irishmen in Belfast. They believed in the ideas of the French Revolution and wanted to make Ireland an independent republic. Their leader was a lawyer from Dublin called Theobald Wolfe Tone. He thought that all Irish people, whatever their religion, could be united together. He also persuaded the French to send troops to support an Irish uprising. However, the uprising in 1798 turned into a war of Catholic against Protestant, with both sides fighting with great cruelty. The uprising was defeated and 30,000 people died. Tone was captured and tried for treason, but he committed suicide in prison before the death sentence could be carried out.

AD 1504 The pocket handkerchief is first used.

AD 1506 The first loads of spices are brought to Europe by sea from the East Indies.

AD 1509 Wallpaper is printed in England. At first it comes only in black and white.

AD 1517 Coffee is drunk in Istanbul for the first time.

AD 1540 Wooden legs are fitted to the limbs of wounded soldiers.

AD 1543 Copernicus describes how the Earth circles around the Sun.

Orange Order

From 1793, Catholics could become lawyers and carry weapons. Dissenters from Ulster Protestants were alarmed by these changes and formed the Orange Order to defend their community. Ulster Catholics formed the Defenders to combat the Orangemen.

Robert Emmet

Robert Emmet, also a Protestant United Irishman, led another failed rebellion in Dublin in 1803. The uprising was crushed after a judge was murdered. Emmet was later hanged.

Union

The 1798 uprising terrified Irish Protestants so much that they voted to give up their own Parliament. An Act of Union was agreed which made Britain and Ireland a single 'United Kingdom', with one Parliament in Westminster. An attempt to give Catholics the right to sit in this Parliament was blocked by King George III, as he believed it would break his coronation oath to keep the country Protestant.

Daniel O'Connell

Daniel O'Connell was a Catholic lawyer. He had lived in France where he saw the bloodshed of the Revolution. He thought the Irish uprising of 1798 was a useless waste of life. In 1823, in an attempt to press peacefully for greater Catholic rights, he founded the Catholic Association. For only a penny a month, collected by Catholic priests, people could join the Association – which they did in their thousands. O'Connell's movement gained such widespread support that Parliament in Westminster at last granted Catholics the right to vote in 1829. Catholics could also become MPs and hold positions in government. O'Connell led a group of 60 Irish MPs and managed to get a law passed that meant that Catholics no longer had to pay taxes to support the Protestant Church of Ireland. These taxes were known as tithes, and were not abolished until nine years later in 1838. However, he could not bring an end to the Union and give Ireland her own parliament again.

AD 1559 The first European encyclopedia is written.

AD 1564 Lead pencils are made using wood and graphite.

AD 1589 William Lee invents the first knitting machine.

AD 1589 Flush toilets with underground sewage tanks are designed.

AD 1590 A microscope is invented in Holland.

AD 1593 Galileo invents the glass thermometer.

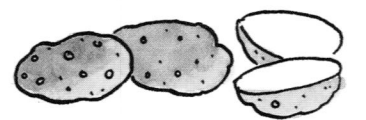 

Famine

During the 1840s, Ireland suffered a terrible disaster when the potato crop failed for four years running. A million people starved or died of disease as a result. Another million were forced to move to different countries.

The potato

By the 1600s, potatoes introduced from South America were being grown in Ireland. They grew well in poor soil and on patches of land too small to grow wheat. Also, the only tool needed to raise potatoes was a spade, so it was the ideal crop for poor people with little land to farm. By 1845, a third of Irish families ate only boiled potatoes served with a little bacon fat or milk.

Disaster!

In 1845, the potato crops were attacked by a fungus which destroyed one third of the plants. Most people had some savings and could buy the maize the British government sent to Ireland in an attempt to stop widespread starvation. In 1846, the potato crop failed again, but this time the situation was worse than the last. People had no savings left to pay for food, so the British government was forced to put people to work mending roads and digging ditches in order that they could earn money to pay for food. Over a million people had to work for the government in this way. However, the taxes needed to pay for these schemes had to be raised in Ireland itself. The 1847 harvest was poor again, partly because people had been forced to eat the potatoes that they would normally have saved for planting the next year. The fungus struck again in 1848.

Landlords

Many landlords tried to help the farmers during the potato famine by not asking for rent so they could buy food instead. However, some landlords forced farmers, who could not pay the rent, off their land, in order to save themselves from ruin. Tens of thousands of starving people were forced to wander the roads, desperately looking for food or work. As they were so weak from hunger, many died from disease.

AD 1600
The recorder becomes popular.

AD 1605 The first regular newspaper appears in Antwerp in Belgium.

AD 1607 The first English settlement is made at Jamestown, Virginia, in North America.

AD 1608 Cheques are used to pay bills for the first time in Holland.

AD 1609 The Dutch East India company ships tea from China to Europe.

AD 1619 African slaves arrive in North America.

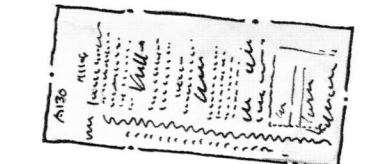

Afterwards

The Irish famine was the worst food crisis in all of Europe during this time. The effect on Ireland was devastating. During the famine, around a million people died and a further million fled overseas (emigrated) to Britain, America, Canada or Australia. The emigration continued even after the famine ended in 1849. In 1841, Ireland had a population of more than eight million people, but by 1881 there was only half that number.

Bitterness

The famine was so widespread that no government at that time could have helped the Irish. However, Britain was at the height of its power and did too little too late to help. Partly, this was a result of ignorance, but mostly it was because it was seen as an Irish problem for the Irish to solve. It is no surprise that the Irish were very bitter about this.

America

During the 1840s, around 780,000 Irish people went to America. Between 1850 and 1930 they were joined by another 4,000,000 of their emigrating countryfolk. Although many of the Irish travelling to America came from rural areas, they tended to live together in large groups in cities, such as New York and Boston, when they arrived. Following O'Connell's example, the Irish formed political groups and organised the local politics in the cities. It was not long before they were becoming important members of society, such as policemen and government officials. Although most people were happy to live in a new country that offered more opportunity than in Ireland, some were still angry about the hardship they had faced back home.

Annie Moore was a typical emigrant. She left Ireland with her two brothers in 1889. You can learn all about her at 'The Queenstown Story' in the Heritage Centre, Cobh, County Cork.

AD 1625 Fire engines are used in London.

AD 1628 William Harvey discovers how blood circulates.

AD 1642 Blaise Pascal invents the first calculator.

AD 1653 The first letter boxes appear in Paris.

AD 1666 The Great Fire of London destroys much of the city.

AD 1677 In Paris, ice cream is eaten for dessert.

Fenians and Ulstermen

The horror of the 1840s forced the Irish to think about a new future for their country. A minority thought that violent revolution was the only answer. Meanwhile, the growth of new industries in Ulster made its Protestant people feel even more different from their more rural Catholic neighbours.

Young Ireland

While Daniel O'Connell had been willing to work through the British Parliament to get reforms for Ireland, some younger Irish people were not. They wanted Ireland to reform itself and restore its national pride. To spread their message they founded a movement called 'Young Ireland' and a successful newspaper called *The Nation*. However, their attempt to start a revolution in 1848 was not so successful and was easily defeated.

JAMES STEPHENS   CARDINAL CULLEN   JOHN O'MAHONY

The Fenians

In 1858, two former members of Young Ireland, James Stephens and John O'Mahony, founded the Irish Republican Brotherhood. Stephens had lived in Paris, where he had been influenced by revolutionaries. O'Mahony lived in New York and was able to raise money and support from the Irish people living there. Their organisation became known as the Fenians, a name taken from the Fianna, heroic warriors of ancient Ireland. The Fenians believed that Ireland should become an independent republic and that the only way to bring this about was by force. Their ideas were strongly opposed by Paul Cardinal Cullen, the Archbishop of Dublin. This opposition from the Catholic Church limited the influence of the Fenians in Ireland itself.

AD 1700 The clarinet is invented.

AD 1709 The first piano is built in Italy.

AD 1712 The first reliable steam engine is invented by Thomas Newcomen in England.

AD 1732 Sleeping powder is invented in England.

AD 1738 Cuckoo clocks appear in the Black Forest region of Germany.

AD 1742 The centigrade scale of temperature is used on a thermometer.

AD 1700   AD 1709   AD 1712   AD 1732   AD 1738   AD 1742

Bombings

In the 1860s, the Fenians organised bombings in England and, from America, armed raids against the British in Canada. Their attempt at an armed rising in Ireland in 1867 failed completely. However, in 1885 they managed to bomb the British House of Commons.

Gladstone, the British Prime Minister, was an important ally in the quest for Home Rule

Industrial Ulster

While most of Ireland starved in the 1840s, modern industry grew rapidly in Ulster. Linen-making, engineering and shipbuilding turned Belfast into a boom city. Protestant businessmen and their skilled workers became much better off than their Catholic neighbours and thought themselves closer to Britain, the world's leading industrial power. From the 1850s onwards, fights between Protestants and Catholics broke out on the streets of Belfast.

Home Rule

Although the Fenians hit the headlines, they had few followers. In the 1870s, Irish MPs in the Parliament in Westminster began to campaign for 'Home Rule'. This meant Ireland would remain part of the United Kingdom but it would have its own parliament to pass its own laws, just as it had done before the 1801 Act of Union.

AD 1752 Benjamin Franklin of the United States invents the lightning conductor.

AD 1767 James Hargreaves invents the Spinning Jenny.

AD 1770 False teeth made from porcelain are used in France.

AD 1783 The Montgolfier brothers of France build the first hot-air balloon.

AD 1789 The French Revolution starts in Paris. People are executed by the guillotine.

AD 1796 A vaccine against smallpox is used by Edward Jenner in England.

Parnell

Alongside the struggle for Home Rule and a better deal for the farmers, there grew a new pride in Irish traditions. However, these changes also threatened to bring the country to the brink of civil war.

The League

Parnell was a Protestant landlord, but he worked closely with Michael Davitt, a Catholic and the son of a poor peasant. Together they founded the Irish National Land League. The League wanted fair rents for the farmer and stronger limits on the power of the landlords to evict tenants.

A new leader

In the 1880s, the Home Rule movement found a tough new leader – Charles Stewart Parnell. He turned the movement into the Irish Parliamentary Party (IPP), a well-organised group which would all vote the same way in the British Parliament.

Land war

During the 1880s a 'land war' raged through the Irish countryside as tenants fought to force landlords and the British government to bring reforms. The tenants burnt down barns, maimed cattle, beat up farm managers and even shot landlords.

Scandal

By 1885, Parnell could command the votes of 85 Irish MPs and was an important figure in the British Parliament. Although an attempt to get Home Rule failed in 1886, it seemed only a matter of time before it would be granted. Then, in 1890, scandalous news broke out – Parnell had been living for years with a married woman called Kitty O'Shea. Parnell lost the support of the Catholic Church and the leadership of the IPP. The struggle to hold on to power broke Parnell and he died the next year.

AD 1800 The first electric battery is made in Italy.

AD 1801 William Symington builds the first successful steamship, called *Charlotte Dundas*, in Scotland.

AD 1807 Gas lamps light up the streets of London at night.

AD 1808 The first mechanical typewriter is built.

AD 1822 Gideon Mantell finds the first dinosaur teeth.

AD 1823 Charles Macintosh of Scotland introduces the waterproof coat.

Home Rule

The Fenian legacy was to keep the revolutionary spirit alive. In 1905, a former Fenian, Arthur Griffith, founded Sinn Féin (Gaelic for 'We Ourselves'). He urged Irish MPs to leave Westminster and set up their own Parliament in Dublin. However, John Redmond, leader of the IPP, had the upper hand. The votes he commanded in Westminster allowed him to do a deal where his support of the Liberal Party would gain Home Rule for Ireland.

Civil war?

Ulster Protestants were against Home Rule as they believed it would lead to complete separation from Britain. About 400,000 people signed a 'Solemn League and Covenant'—a promise that they would resist Home Rule, by force if necessary. However, by the time the Home Rule Bill was passed in 1914, Europe was plunged into a world war. The future of Ireland was set aside as thousands of Irishmen of all religions volunteered to fight Germany.

Irish pride

While Parnell was strengthening Irish political power, scholars were strengthening traditional Irish culture. They promoted the Gaelic language, interest in Irish legends and history, and the writing of new poetry and plays. In 1884, the Gaelic Athletic Association (GAA) was founded to revive interest in traditional sports, such as Gaelic football and hurling. The GAA soon attracted many people who wanted an independent Ireland. Going to watch a 'foreign' sport, such as soccer or cricket, was enough to get a person banned from the GAA. This revival of Irish culture by the Catholic majority widened the gap with the Ulster Protestants, who took pride in their link with Britain.

AD 1827 The first photograph is taken in France.

AD 1829 Louis Braille introduces his system of raised dots to allow blind people to read with their fingers.

AD 1829 A sewing machine is built in France.

AD 1839 The bicycle with pedals is invented.

AD 1839 Baseball is first played in America.

AD 1840 Postage stamps begin to be used on letters.

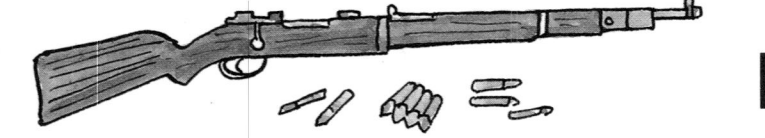

Rebellion!

In 1916, there was a rebellion in Dublin. Although the rebellion was defeated, the events afterwards ensured that it would be one of the most important milestones in the struggle for Irish freedom.

John Redmond

National Volunteers

In return for Home Rule, Redmond promised to support Britain during the war. However, his promise split the Irish Volunteers, a militia or small armed force, set up to oppose the threat to conscription. Most stayed loyal to Redmond, calling themselves National Volunteers. The rest kept the old name and thought Britain's quarrel with Germany was no business of Ireland's.

Conspiracy

Within the ranks of the Irish Volunteers was a small, secret band of Fenians. Led by the poet and teacher, Patrick Pearse, they thought that while Britain was distracted by war, there was a perfect chance to start a rising for Irish independence. They sent messengers to Germany to get weapons, and joined forces with James Connolly, the leader of a small militia, the Irish Citizen Army.

The Easter Rising

On Easter Monday, 24 April 1916, the Fenians seized a number of public buildings in Dublin. They made the General Post Office in O'Connell Street their headquarters, hoisted a tricolour flag and read out a proclamation to establish a Republic of Ireland. The rebels fought bravely but were bound to be defeated once the British recovered from their total surprise. A British gunboat sailed up the River Liffey to bombard the city into surrender. The fighting was over in a week.

AD 1851 Double-decker buses are used in London.

AD 1855 David Livingstone crosses Africa and discovers the Victoria Falls.

AD 1857 The first elevator is put into a department store in America.

AD 1857 Work starts on a trans-Atlantic cable for sending telegraph messages from Europe to America.

AD 1859 Work starts on the Suez Canal.

AD 1861 Daily weather forecasts start in Britain.

Martyrs

As far as the British were concerned, the Rising was an act of treachery and they executed 16 of the leaders. However, Redmond, George Bernard Shaw (the famous Irish playwright), and the Bishop of Limerick all protested against the executions, which seemed cruel and useless once the Rising had been put down. The support of the Bishop of Limerick was important as it changed years of hostility to the Fenians by the Catholic Church. To millions of Irish people, Pearse and his comrades became heroes and martyrs to a great cause – the freedom of Ireland.

British blunders

The British mistakenly blamed Sinn Féin for the events of 1916. They later made the bigger mistake of threatening to force Irishmen to join the army and fight in the war. This was bitterly opposed by Sinn Féin, now under the leadership of Eamon de Valera, the senior survivor of the Rising. It was also opposed by the Catholic Church, the IPP, the IRB and the GAA. Nationalist Ireland was uniting ever more strongly against British rule.

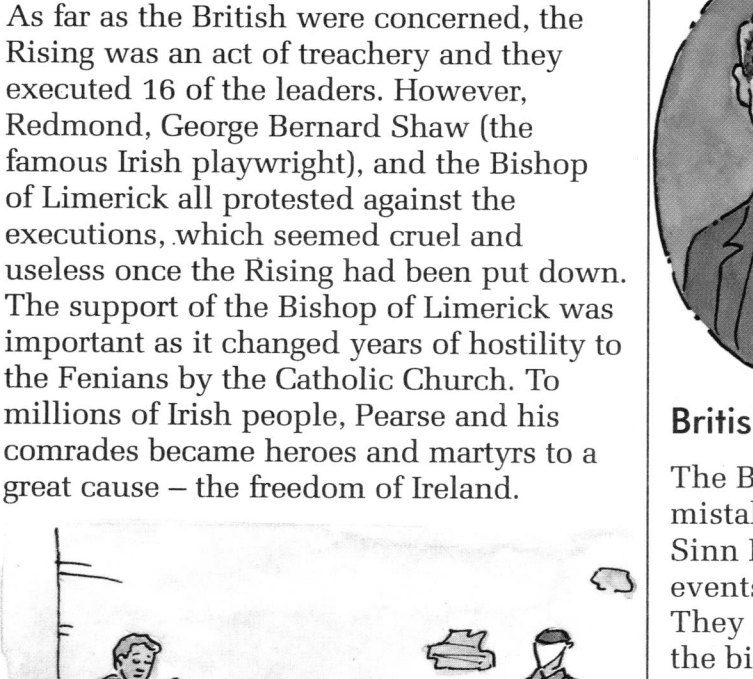

VOTE FOR de VALERA
The Man in Jail for Ireland.
SINN FÉIN

The war of independence

When the war ended in 1918, an election was held. Ulster Protestants voted for continued union with Britain. Sinn Féin won almost every other seat in the rest of Ireland. Rather than go to Westminster, Sinn Féin's 73 MPs met in Dublin on 21 January 1919 as Dáil Eireann (the Assembly of Ireland). On the same day, two members of the Irish Volunteers (now called the Irish Republican Army) shot two policemen. For the next two and a half years, the IRA fought British troops and police in hundreds of small-scale ambushes and shoot-outs.

AD 1863 Roller skating becomes very popular in America.

AD 1864 The Red Cross is set up.

AD 1877 Public telephones appear in the USA.

AD 1895 The first cinema is opened by the Lumière brothers.

AD 1895 The safety razor is invented by Gillette.

AD 1896 The first modern Olympics are held in Greece.

The outbreaks of violence led to the establishment of two separate Irish governments – and more troubles.

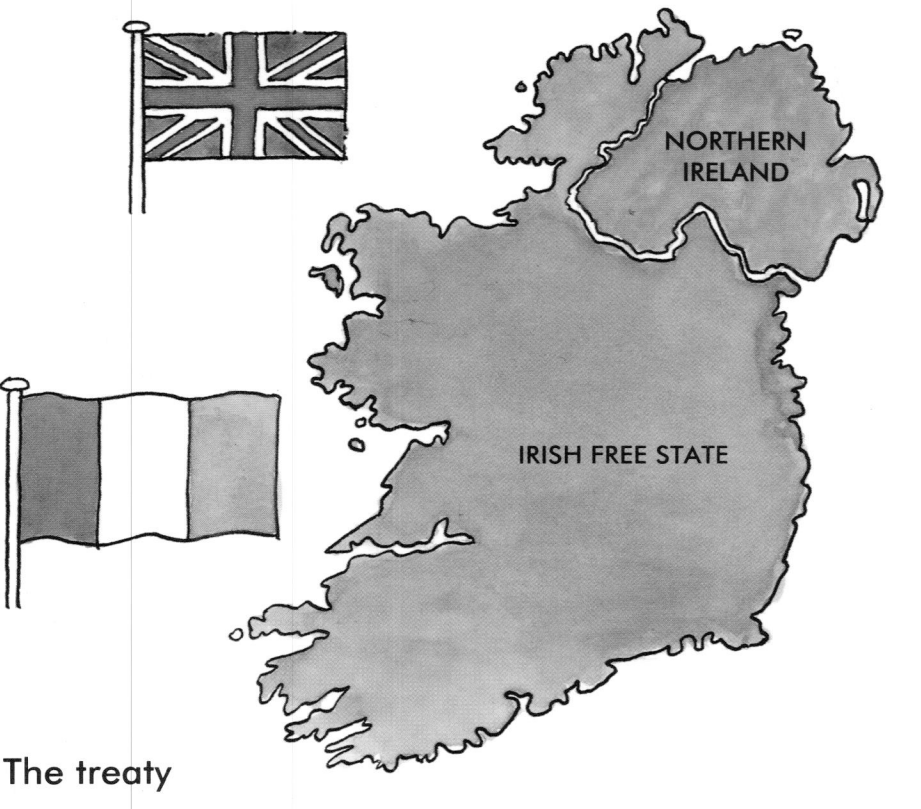

The treaty

In 1921, two years of vicious fighting ended in a truce and a treaty. The British realised that the Nationalists (those who wanted an independent Ireland) in the South could not be defeated and that the Unionists in the North would not accept separation from Britain. The treaty was signed in London and resulted in the 26 southern counties becoming the 'Irish Free State' – a dominion, like Canada or Australia. This meant that Southern Ireland would be an independent country under its own government, but with the British monarch as the head of state and symbol of Irish loyalty. Meanwhile, in a separate development, Ireland was divided. The six northern counties got their own form of Home Rule within the Union. This division of Ireland was called Partition.

Civil war

The Anglo-Irish treaty of 1921 was agreed by Arthur Griffith, deputy leader of Sinn Féin, and Michael Collins, a brilliant young IRA commander. A small majority of the Dáil and the Irish people were ready to accept the settlement, but de Valera and his supporters were not. The IRA and Sinn Féin split and another civil war – between Irish Nationalists – was fought over the treaty. Both Griffith and Collins were killed. The side in favour of the treaty won.

Right: Arthur Griffith and Michael Collins

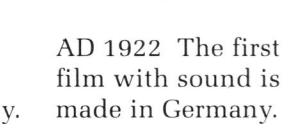

AD 1901 A radio message is sent across the Atlantic by the Italian inventor Guglielmo Marconi.

AD 1903 The Wright brothers fly the first aeroplane.

AD 1903 The teddy bear is invented. It is named after the American President Teddy Roosevelt.

AD 1914 The First World War begins. It ends in 1918. At least 10 million people are killed.

AD 1921 Motorways are built in Germany.

AD 1922 The first film with sound is made in Germany.

De Valera

De Valera returned to power in 1932, as head of a new political party, Fianna Fáil. As Taoiseach, and later as President, he remained active in politics until 1973. In 1937, under his leadership Ireland adopted a new constitution, or set of rules, which broke the link with the British crown as the head of state of Ireland.

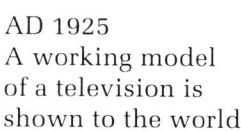

Ulster

While independent Ireland was gradually developing its own separate character, Northern Ireland held firm to the Unionist link. Thanks to its industries, it was more properous than its southern neighbour. However, the prosperity was not equally shared. Two-thirds of the population were Protestants, and their leaders used their control of local government and business to deny Catholics a fair share of the jobs and housing, paid for out of taxes. Many Catholics looked south for support of their rights. Some thought that justice could only be achieved if Partition was ended and Ireland was united as a single country.

Republic

Ireland remained neutral during World War II, though many Irishmen did fight for the British army. In 1949, it ended its last political link with Britain by withdrawing from the Commonwealth and declaring itself to be the 'Republic of Ireland'.

AD 1925
A working model of a television is shown to the world.

AD 1937
The jet engine is designed.

AD 1939 The Second World War begins. It ends in 1945. Between 35 and 60 million people are killed.

AD 1940 The first helicopter flight ends safely.

AD 1942 A small nuclear reactor is tested - it works.

AD 1946
The world's first computer is built in the USA.

The road ahead

The 1960s saw a new outbreak of armed conflict to end the partition of Ireland. The 1990s saw a new hope – that a way forward could be found through peace.

Looking outward

After the ending of World War II, more and more Irish people began to emigrate from the Republic in search of work. Ireland needed to create new jobs and more modern industries. In the 1960s, Ireland began to enjoy greater prosperity as foreign companies set up factories there. In 1973, Ireland joined the European Economic Community (EEC).

New troubles

During the 1950s and 1960s, black people in the US struggled to gain equal rights with white people. Their movement was copied by Catholics in Northern Ireland. In 1968, demonstrations began, demanding fair treatment for housing and employment. Protestants were afraid that the cry for civil rights would turn into a demand for an end to the Union with Britain and the creation of a single Ireland. Civil rights meetings led to fights between Catholics and Protestants. Many Catholics did not trust the police, who were almost all Protestants, to protect them and keep the peace.

Troops in

In 1969, the British government ordered soldiers to patrol the streets of Belfast and Derry to keep Catholics and Protestants apart. At first, Catholics welcomed the troops as defenders. However, the IRA soon saw a chance to join the conflict. They claimed to defend Catholics from harassment by Protestants, police or troops, but were soon on the offensive with a campaign of bombing and shooting, both in Ulster and on the British mainland. This was intended to force the British government to withdraw its troops and give up supporting the position of Northern Ireland as part of the United Kingdom.

AD 1953 Mount Everest, the world's highest mountain, is climbed.

AD 1955 The design for a hovercraft is finished.

AD 1961 Russia sends a man into space.

AD 1963 Cassette tapes are sold.

AD 1969 American astronauts land on the Moon.

AD 1971 Video cassette recorders are sold.

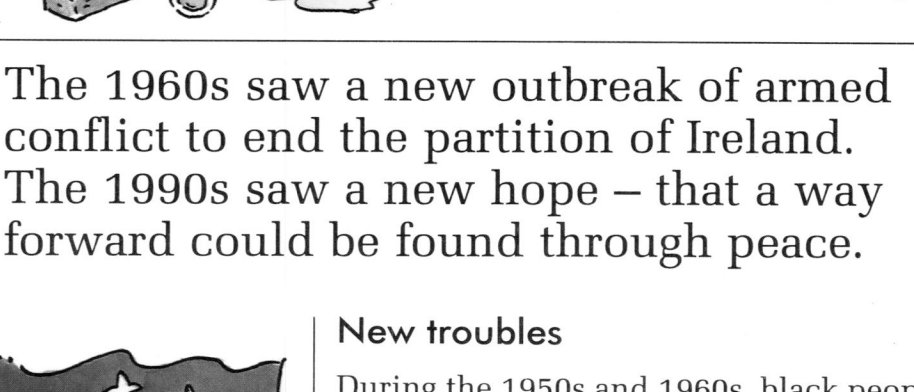

AD 1953
AD 1955
AD 1961
AD 1963
AD 1969
AD 1971

Violence

The IRA campaign went on for 25 years. Some Protestants formed armed militias to fight back with their own campaign of bombing and shooting. In all, more than 3,000 people were killed, many of them children. Many people on both sides supported peace movements to end the violence, but the two communities remained divided by separate schooling, housing and even sports.

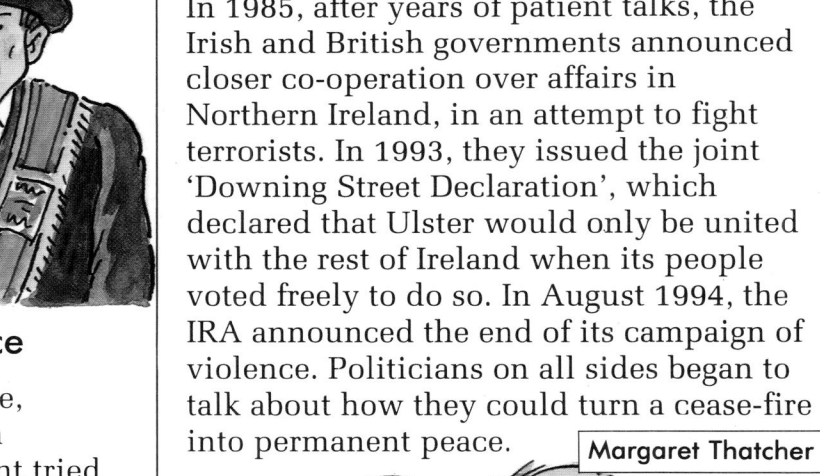

Resistance

Meanwhile, the British government tried to find a peaceful end to the conflict. Northern Ireland's Parliament, which had ruled unfairly over Catholics, was suspended in favour of direct rule from London. Unfair treatment of Catholics over jobs and housing was made illegal. However, an attempt to introduce a new form of government which would share power between Protestants and Catholics was defeated by a huge Protestant strike in 1974.

Troops out?

In 1985, after years of patient talks, the Irish and British governments announced closer co-operation over affairs in Northern Ireland, in an attempt to fight terrorists. In 1993, they issued the joint 'Downing Street Declaration', which declared that Ulster would only be united with the rest of Ireland when its people voted freely to do so. In August 1994, the IRA announced the end of its campaign of violence. Politicians on all sides began to talk about how they could turn a cease-fire into permanent peace.

Margaret Thatcher

John Major

Garret FitzGerald

Charles Haughey

Albert Reynolds

Gerry Adams

Peter Brooke

John Hume

AD 1972 Pocket calculators are sold.

AD 1977 Personal computers for use at home and in the office are invented.

AD 1978 The first test-tube baby, called Louise Brown, is born.

AD 1979 Personal stereos are sold.

AD 1981 The first space shuttle, *Columbia*, is launched.

AD 1991 Virtual reality games are introduced.

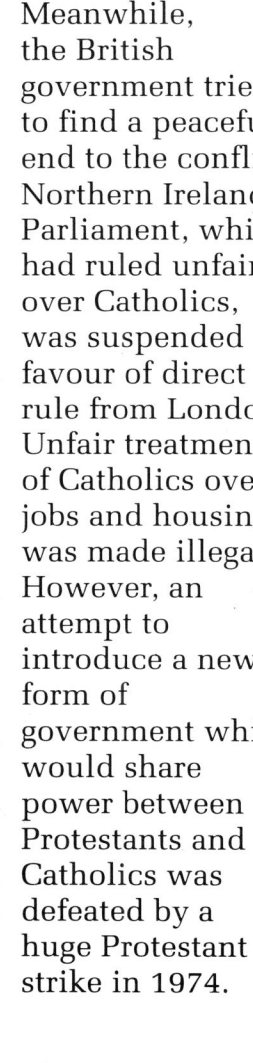

Index

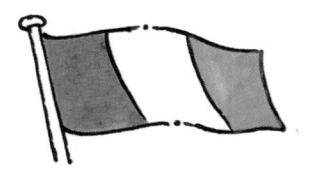